BLESSED BY LIGHT

BLESSED BY LIGHT

VISIONS OF THE COLORADO PLATEAU

EDITED BY STEPHEN TRIMBLE
FOREWORD BY EDWARD ABBEY
INTRODUCTION BY GIBBS M. SMITH

➜P

GIBBS M. SMITH, INC.
PEREGRINE SMITH BOOKS

This is a Peregrine Smith Book
Copyright © 1986 by Gibbs M. Smith, Inc.

All rights reserved: no portion of this book may be used or reproduced without written permission from the publisher, with the exception of brief passages for review purposes

Published by Gibbs M. Smith, Inc., P.O. Box 667, Layton, Utah 84041

Printed and bound in Japan

90 89 88 87 86   5 4 3 2 1

First Edition

Book design by J. Scott Knudsen

Cover photograph by Tom Till: Grand Canyon of the Colorado

Library of Congress Cataloging-in-Publication Data

Blessed by light.

    ''Peregrine Smith books.''
    Bibliography: p.
    1. Colorado Plateau—Description and travel—Views.
I. Trimble, Stephen A.
F788.B64 1986 979.1'3
86-6740
ISBN 0-87905-236-8

TO THIS END, MY FATHERS,
MY CHILDREN
MAY ALL OF YOU BE BLESSED WITH LIGHT

PRAYER OF THE ZUNI FIREKEEPER AT WINTER SOLSTICE

Tom Bean: moonrise over Vishnu Temple, Grand Canyon.

The canyon country of southern Utah and northern Arizona—the Colorado Plateau—is something special. Something strange, marvelous, full of wonders. As far as I know there is no other region on earth much like it, or even remotely like it. Nowhere else have we had this lucky combination of vast sedimentary rock formations exposed to a desert climate, a great plateau carved by major rivers—the Green, the San Juan, the Colorado—into such a surreal land of form and color. Add a few volcanoes, the standing necks of which can still be seen, and cinder cones and lava flows, and at least four separate laccolithic mountain ranges nicely distributed about the region, and more hills, holes, humps and hollows, reefs, folds, salt domes, swells and grabens, buttes, benches and mesas, synclines, monoclines, and anticlines than you can ever hope to see and explore in one lifetime, and you begin to arrive at an approximate picture of the plateau's surface appearance.

. . . And yet—when all we know about it is said and measured and tabulated, there remains something in the soul of the place, the spirit of the whole, that cannot be fully assimilated by the human imagination."

Edward Abbey, *The Journey Home*

We are grateful to the following writers and publishers for permission to reprint quotations from their work:

Edward Abbey: for quotations from his books *Desert Solitaire, Slickrock, The Monkey Wrench Gang, The Journey Home,* and *Beyond the Wall.* Copyright by Edward Abbey. Reprinted by permission.

University of Arizona Press, Tucson: *The Land of Journeys' Ending* by Mary Austin. Copyright 1983 by the University of Arizona Press; *A Canyon Voyage: The Narrative of the Second Powell Expedition Down the Colorado River from Wyoming, and the Explorations, in the Years 1871 and 1872* by Frederick S. Dellenbaugh. Copyright 1984 by the University of Arizona Press. Reprinted by permission.

Colorado National Monument Association, Fruita, Colorado: *Rim of Time: The Canyons of Colorado National Monument* by Stephen Trimble. Copyright 1979 by Colorado National Monument Association. Reprinted by permission.

Crown Publishers Inc., New York: *Anasazi: Ancient People of the Rock* by Donald G. Pike, 1974. Reprinted by permission.

E.P. Dutton, New York: *Listen, Bright Angel* by Edwin Corle. Copyright 1946 by Edwin Corle. Reprinted by permission.

Farrar, Straus & Giroux, Inc., New York: *Encounters With the Archdruid* by John McPhee. Copyright 1971 by John McPhee. Originally appeared in *The New Yorker.* Reprinted by permission.

Zane Grey, Inc.: *Riders of the Purple Sage* by Zane Grey. Harper & Row, New York, 1915. Reprinted by permission.

Harper & Row, Publishers, Inc., New York: *Wind in the Rock* by Ann Zwinger. Copyright 1978 by Ann Zwinger. Reprinted by permission.

Houghton Mifflin Company, Boston: *The Song of the Lark* by Willa Cather. Copyright 1915 and 1943 by Willa Siebert Cather. Reprinted by permission.

Alfred A. Knopf, Inc., New York: *The Professor's House* by Willa Cather, copyright 1925 by Willa Cather and renewed 1953 by Edith Lewis and the City Bank Farmers Trust Company; *Death Comes for the Archbishop* by Willa Cather, copyright 1927 by Willa Cather and renewed 1955 by The Executors of the Estate of Willa Cather; and *The Man Who Walked Through Time* by Colin Fletcher, copyright 1967 by Colin Fletcher. The above reprinted by permission of Alfred A. Knopf, Inc.

David Lavender: *One Man's West* by David Lavender. Doubleday & Company, New York, 1956. Reprinted by permission.

Anton V. Long: *Piñon Country* by Haniel Long, Duell, Sloan & Pearce, 1941. Copyright 1969 by Anton V. Long; Copyright 1975 with preface by Fray Angelico Chavez, Sunstone Press, Santa Fe, New Mexico. Reprinted by permission.

Barry Lopez: *River Notes: The Dance of Herons* by Barry Lopez, Andrews and McMeel, Kansas City, 1979; ''Into the Earth'' by Barry Lopez, *Plateau Magazine: Water on the Plateau,* Museum of Northern Arizona Press, 1981. Reprinted by permission.

N. Scott Momaday: *The Names* by N. Scott Momaday, Harper & Row, New York, 1976. Reprinted by permission.

Museum of Northern Arizona Press, Flagstaff: *The Bright Edge: A Guide to the National Parks of the Colorado Plateau* by Stephen Trimble. Copyright 1979 by Museum of Northern Arizona Press. Reprinted by permission.

Ohio University Press, Athens, Ohio: *The Colorado* by Frank Waters. Ohio University Press, 1985. Reprint of 1974 Holt, Rinehart & Winston edition. Reprinted by permission.

University of Oklahoma Press: *Down the Colorado* by Robert Brewster Stanton, edited and with an Introduction by Dwight L. Smith. Copyright 1965 by the University of Oklahoma Press. Reprinted by permission.

A.D. Peters & Co. Ltd, London: *Midnight On the Desert* by J.B. Priestley. Reader's Union Limited & William Heinemann Limited, London, 1940. Reprinted by permission.

University of Pittsburgh Press: *A Western Journal: A Daily Log of the Great Parks Trip, June 20-July 2, 1938* by Thomas Wolfe. University of Pittsburgh Press. Copyright 1967 by Paul Gitlin, Administrator, C.T.A. Reprinted by permission.

G.P. Putnam's Sons, New York: *Canyon Country* by Julius F. Stone. Copyright 1932 by Julius F. Stone. Reprinted by permission.

The Rio Grande Press, Inc., Glorieta, New Mexico 87535: *To the Foot of the Rainbow* by Clyde Kluckhohn. Rio Grande Press edition published in 1980. Reprinted by permission.

Rock Point Community School and Mr. George Blueeyes of the Navajo Nation, Arizona: Poem by George Blueeyes on page 2 of *Between Sacred Mountains,* Rock Point Community School, 1982. Reprinted by permission.

Charles Scribner's Sons, New York: *The Grand Canyon of the Colorado* by John C. Van Dyke. Copyright 1920 by John C. Van Dyke. Reprinted by permission.

Gibbs M. Smith, Inc., Salt Lake City: *Scenes in America Deserta* by Reyner Banham, 1982; *The Place No One Knew: Glen Canyon on the Colorado River* by Eliot Porter; *Everett Ruess: A Vagabond for Beauty* by W.L. Rusho, 1983. Reprinted by permission.

Wallace Stegner: *The Sound of Mountain Water* by Wallace Stegner, Doubleday & Company, New York, 1969; *American Places* by Wallace Stegner, Greenwich House, New York, 1983. Reprinted by permission.

L.E. Stevens/Red Lake Books, P.O. Box 1315, Flagstaff, AZ 86002: ''A Boatman's Lessons'' by Larry Stevens, *Plateau Magazine: Water on the Plateau,* Museum of Northern Arizona Press, 1981. Reprinted by permission.

Stewart, Tabori & Chang, New York: Canyonlands National Park chapter by Stephen Trimble in *The Sierra Club Guide to the National Parks of the Desert Southwest* published by Stewart, Tabori & Chang, 1984. Reprinted by permission.

Paul G. Zolbrod: *Diné Bahane': The Navajo Creation Story* by Paul G. Zolbrod. Copyright 1984 by the University of New Mexico Press. Reprinted by permission.

CONTENTS

Steve McDowell: cottonwood leaves and drying silt, San Rafael Swell, Utah.

INTRODUCTION
HOMELAND

The Colorado Plateau selects its people. If chosen you know: this landscape speaks to your emotions and spirit. You belong. Contact with this place refreshes and rejuvenates; it can even be an erotic experience to discover yourself so attracted and sustained by a landscape.

The photographs and literary expressions in this book have been created by people who have been able to transcend the literal and respond to the spirit of the plateau. The photographers represented here are a new generation of plateau appreciators. Their work captures a new vision of the region. These photographs carry a rich load of information about the land and the human spirit in our time. Everything these men and women know about themselves and the land is distilled in these photographs. The writers represented here come from the small band who have succeeded in the past century in symbolizing the landscape of the plateau in literature.

The Colorado Plateau encompasses 130,000 square miles in southern Utah, western Colorado, northern Arizona and northwest New Mexico. Elevation ranges from below 2,000 to well over 12,000 feet, mostly high desert between 4,500 and 7,000 feet.

The heart of the Colorado Plateau for me is in southeastern Utah's red rock canyon country, a region largely unexplored until the 1950s, a remnant of Wild America. When Robert Marshall, while working for the Forest Service in 1936, made a survey of the remaining roadless areas in America, the largest single intact area was in southeastern Utah and northern Arizona—10,820,000 acres without roads. Since then the area has been penetrated by highways, harnessed with dams and power plants, and developed for minerals—yet one of the powerful attractions of this land is still its wildness.

There are no major urban centers in the heartland of the Colorado Plateau. Most people live on its fringe. To get to know the plateau, one must be willing to get out of the automobile and walk and camp. Here you can still find lifegiving solitude—a place where you can experience the intimate peace of our natural home. Henry Thoreau seemed to be describing this region when he talked of "This vast, savage, howling mother of ours lying all around, with such Beauty and such affection for her children."

There are two ways to experience the plateau country. One is to enter the canyons—to go down, become immersed and swallowed and consumed in a canyon. To be overwhelmed by soaring 3,000-foot walls of sandstone; to squeeze through narrow labyrinthine slots, float down the river gorges; to let the land mold you, scrape you, buffet you physically and emotionally and thereby refresh you.

Most canyons on the plateau have some things in common—similar erosion patterns, plant life, colors and rock types and formations. Yet each canyon and gulch has its own personality—its intimate heart which can be known by spending time there camping and by walking its length. In the canyon there are continually new experiences to keep you focused. Around each bend the light changes, the cliffs change, the coyote's tail swishes around the curve ahead. There is adventure and variety and your mind attends. You observe the particular, the specific place. You feel at home; you belong there in the canyon focused and at peace and entertained by the variety. You get to know the canyon and feel its personality. It is an intimate experience. One must know canyons to know the Colorado Plateau.

The second path to understanding this country is to gain a perch on high ground to assimilate the grand view and find perspective, to allow your eye and mind to penetrate and become immersed. I feel one must earn this experience. Knowing the canyons must come first; without that apprenticeship the view from the high ground is only another view. With knowledge of the canyons this view is transformed into a profound experience.

Four high vantage points on the plateau have special meaning to me. One is a point on the Aquarius Plateau (Boulder Mountain) at around 8,000 feet. Looking south the Henry Mountains are to the left, on the right is the long, flat arc of the Kaiparowits Plateau. Straight ahead I can gaze 100 miles south across the broken Escalante plain into the blue northern shadow of Navajo Mountain. Knowing the gulches, washes and canyons of the Escalante country—Harris, Coyote, Davis, Cottonwood, and many more—makes this view a profound experience. From this vantage I always feel the power and spirit of the Colorado Plateau.

Another is a high camp in Arizona on Tsegi Mesa, its canyons honeycombed with Anasazi cliff dwellings. It is a place where two great cobalt-blue sacred flat-topped humps can be seen and felt: the enormous piñon- and juniper-covered shapes of Black Mesa to the east, and, in the west and farther away, the ponderosa-forested Kaibab Plateau. Nowhere else do I feel the spirit of ancient and contemporary Indian America as strongly.

Then there is a windblown camp on a large towering rock next to a piñon bonsai at the edge of the Grand Canyon at Toroweap. Here one can gaze 3,000 feet down into the Colorado River. At night one can hear when the breeze blows just right muffled sounds filtering up from the chasm—a gentle roar from Lava Falls and, miraculously, a garbled word or two from the river runners gathered around campfires, firefly specks far below. There is a strong feeling of security here on the edge: a balance between the immensity of the plateau and the smallness of humans.

Finally there is an old cowboy cabin high in the La Sal Mountains, built in the 1920s and filled with camping and kitchen supplies from the past. From here you can look south to the Blue Mountains, west across Canyonlands, and north on Arches National Park and out beyond to the Book Cliffs. The High Plateaus, central backbone of Utah and the western edge of the Colorado Plateau, are in the farthest, most dim distance. From here the yellows, reds, pinks, roses, and blues of the canyons and the desert fill the entire atmosphere with rarified and refracted light and color. Often there are the slanting lines of rain, walking, performing. The scene is always alive and animated, full of energy for me, the epitome of the dynamism of the entire plateau.

I have noticed the effect of the plateau in sustaining certain individuals beyond their material needs. I have known a few people who have spent their lives elsewhere, and when old, chosen to settle on this land where they have become refreshed and have done amazing things—I believe because they felt nourished by this land's power.

I have known people searching for meaning and identity to come to this wild land and find what they sought. The dramatic plateau landscape best meets their needs to test and risk and expend heightened, focused bursts of energy.

But the most profound human reaction I sense is the feeling of belonging to this land, the feeling of having an intimate relationship with a rugged, wild landscape.

Usually I feel disappointed with what people have done on the plateau. Until very recently the primary human effort here has been to extract minerals or timber or to use the land for grazing animals. But increasingly, we are beginning to recognize recreation and wilderness values.

I am shocked at how poorly modern manmade structures reflect the spirit of this land. Architecture, one of the best ways we have to interpret the aura of landscape, is woefully inadequate here. The plateau needs an important new architecture, belonging to and emerging from this land—as the Pueblo Indian architecture has done for a thousand years. Perhaps the new architecture could build on and be inspired by this tradition.

The rich and stimulating human diversity on the Colorado Plateau has the potential, I believe, when combined with an economic base founded on recreation and preservation of wilderness values, to create new cultural vitality for the region. There is a strong residue—in the land, in the air, and in the rivers—of the Indians' effort to harmonize human existence with this land and the cosmos. The Spanish influence is also evident throughout the Colorado Plateau, especially in its place names dating from the seventeenth, eighteenth, and nineteenth centuries. All over the plateau the aspen trees bear names carved by Spanish and Basque sheepherders in the 1920s, 1930s, and 1940s. And the Mormon settlement of the Colorado Plateau has left a legacy of place names, old adobe and sandstone houses, wide streets with the incongruous look of New England, and large, modern churches.

Millions of people living around its flanks use the plateau in many ways: as a place from which to extract the earth's riches, as a place to explore and to live, and also as a spiritual home, as a place to worship and refresh oneself. It seems even in our materialistic and secular culture we have come to recognize the higher use and value of the plateau: it contains the largest concentration of national parks anywhere in the forty-eight contiguous states. Yet there remains much more land on the plateau that deserves to be protected in wilderness areas or national parks.

We have chosen the photographs and words in this book for their eloquence; they express the unique quality of the Colorado Plateau landscape and light. They speak to the best in us all. For our generation of Americans has one last opportunity to preserve massive tracts of the plateau as wilderness, to keep its wild, ancient pulse strong and sending vitality to all parts of our land. The wild land of the plateau is truly a national treasure. Listen to this land and be proud. Care about it. And act to preserve it as wilderness.

Gibbs M. Smith

FOREWORD

It is difficult to write about the landscape of the American West without lurching into rhapsody, as the testimonials in this book naively demonstrate. And probably no part of that landscape has provoked more rhapsodical prose, purple as the bloom of the sage, than what geographers call the Colorado Plateau province—i.e., the region drained by the Colorado River. For example, any author capable of typing such a phrase as '' . . . the light that never was is here, now, in the storm-sculptured gorge of the Escalante,'' should probably have his typewriter confiscated, hammered flat, and sunk in the silty depths of Lake Powell National Sewage Lagoon. With the author's neck attached by a short length of anchor chain.

This straining after mystical, visionary, transcendental typing has long been a source of amusement to critics and book reviewers among our East Coast literati. (That little clique and claque of prep-school playmates and Ivy League colleagues.) In the minds of those stern-disciplined fellows, with their faces still set toward New England, Old England, central France and the mud of Mississippi, the extravagant language employed by Western writers when writing about the American West reveals a softening of intellect, brain cells addled by too much sun, the lingering afterglow from the sunset of nineteenth century romanticism.

Could be. Maybe they know what they're talking about. But they don't know what we are talking about. We, that is, who live in the West, love the West, hate the West, and persist in trying to paint it, photograph it, and describe its disturbing shapes, colors, and nature through the inadequate vocabulary of a language that was formed among the vapid bogs and insipid fuzzy hills of little England.

It cannot be done. The world is bigger than we are, fundamentally mysterious—why should *anything* exist?—and beyond the scope of human expression. No system of symbols can be expected to comprehend and apprehend that which is the source of all systems. Nevertheless we keep trying, groping, searching, feeling our way toward some sort of vision, some kind of understanding. In the process we are forced to expand the powers of imagination and stretch to breaking point the modes of communication. We always fail, we inevitably look ridiculous. The most heroic efforts lead only to another painting, another photograph, one more book. The best of these refer, finally, only to themselves.

Art cannot replicate the natural world—neither the starry universe nor the voodoo gulches and hoodoo rocks of the canyon country, the high mesas, the sunken rivers, the corroded cliffs of the Colorado Plateau. But these failures do not matter. Not if they result in books worth reading, paintings worth hanging on a wall, or photographs that command more than a caption, more than one passive look. The purpose of art is not replication but creation—the making of integrated little worlds within the greater world that encloses us.

Given that understanding, we can proceed to my second argument. It is not enough to describe the world of nature; the point is to preserve it. It is not enough to paint, photograph, or even to understand the American West; the point is to save it. It is not enough to admire or love the Colorado Plateau region; the point is to defend it from its enemies. Landscape aesthetes are common as lichens on an academic wall. What we need are heroes and heroines—about a million of them—willing and able to fight for the health of the land and its native inhabitants.

The world of Glen Canyon, now buried under the sludge and stagnant waters of Lake Powell, will serve as one good example of what happens when we compromise away too much. The Mojave Desert of southern California—smogged over by urbanization, bombarded by the military, devastated by weekend hordes of mechanical recreationists—is another. I'm hardly thinking of ''wilderness,'' which barely survives in the forty-eight states, but simply of back country, primitive country, of land not yet wholly surrendered to industrialism and industrial tourism. I mean country like the Colorado Plateau, with its many millions of acres of still roadless territory.

Difficulty of access is the most democratic of screening devices. Anyone with the price of an old pickup truck in his bank account is free to explore and enjoy the back country of Utah, Arizona, the Four Corners—few things could be simpler, easier, cheaper. Dirt roads ''lock out'' only those people who fear dust, who cannot cope with a flat tire, who lack the sense to stash a little food, water, and a bedroll in the cargo space of the machine they drive and are driven by—those in short who lack, not money, but *interest*.

The same principle applies to what we loosely call ''wilderness,'' meaning an area without permanent vehicular roads. Any man or woman in normal health, with the price of a pair of walking shoes in his or her pocket, is free to enter, to wander through, to get lost in, and to escape from the easy-going wilderness of the canyonlands. This form of mild adventure has become so popular now that in many places (such as Yosemite, Grand Gulch, the Grand Canyon) a walk in the wilds is subject to permits, advance reservations—rationing.

Which means, to my mind, that we will soon need far more, not less, official wilderness in our United States. More wilderness or fewer people. Preferably both.

The human animal needs adventure. Fantasy is not enough. But more important than our need for open space, physical freedom, occasional solitude, is the need for the land to be let alone and left alone. For its own sake. *Let being be,* said the philosopher Martin Heidegger. I can imagine a civilization wise and generous enough to set aside vast tracts of land where, by mutual agreement, none of us humans enter at all. Ever. A place where our feathered, furred and scaly-skinned cousins—as well as the plants and the rocks—are free to work out their evolutionary destinies without any meddling or ''management'' whatsoever.

Another fantasy, no doubt. Meanwhile, we must begin where we are, with our backs to the wall. Somehow, now or never, we must draw a line before the advance of commercial greed, industrial expansion and population increase and announce, in plain language, ''Enough is enough. Thus far and no farther. Think of your children. Of their children. Of the hawks, buzzards, lizards, bear. Save a little room and time for the free play of the human spirit and the wild play of the animal kingdom.''

I can think of no better place to draw that line—in words of flame, in deeds of conviction—than around the red rock, the sunburnt canyons, the lonesome junipers and the solitary mountain lion of the Colorado Plateau.

Come on in and see for yourself.

Edward Abbey

The United States Congress, through the Bureau of Land Management, is currently conducting a review of all BLM lands in the Plateau to decide which lands will be preserved as wilderness. This is a public political process. You can help.

Write to your senators and congressmen, the BLM, and the conservation organizations listed below and be counted as a person who supports wilderness designation of large portions of the Colorado Plateau. As a demonstration of our concern, the publishers of this book will contribute one dollar for each copy sold to an environmental fund, to aid in the effort to establish and preserve wilderness areas on the Colorado Plateau.

The Sierra Club
730 Polk Avenue
San Francisco, CA 94109

National Audubon Society
950 Third Avenue
New York, NY 10022

The Wilderness Society
1400 Eye Street, NW
Washington, DC 20005

National Parks & Conservation Association
1701 18th Street, NW
Washington, DC 20009

Southern Utah Wilderness Alliance
Box 347
Springdale, UT 84767

Utah Wilderness Association
455 East 400 South #40
Salt Lake City, UT 84111

Utah Wilderness Coalition
P.O. Box 11446
Salt Lake City, Utah 84147

ROCK

"The scene is one of naked rock, the only signs of life being a few stunted shrubs. Here is nothing restful, nothing of the mellow loveliness which characterizes the ordinary landscape. The scene is hard, weird, and fascinating in its strangeness. It stimulates the observer in a strange way. He is tempted to exertion beyond his strength. He must needs see what is beyond, and then what is still beyond, until his strength is gone."
Julius Stone, *Canyon Country*, 1932

"We pushed through maze after maze of bristling rock which the wind had carved into whorls, turrets, windows, and arches of complex design. Wide, flat-bottomed valleys bordered by abrupt walls ran every which way. They crossed each other, paralleled each other, started and stopped with no apparent excuse. You enter the head of one—or the foot; the distinction is meaningless, for they are apt to slope either way at any given point—you follow it several miles and suddenly it ends in a blank cliff. . . .

You can see most anything there in the heart of the Needles. Sharp monoliths leap hundreds of feet into the hard blue sky. Serrated ridges of flaming rock twist in all directions. We picked out figures resembling elephants, sphinxes, battleships, men, shoes, organs and choirs, gargoyles, and what not, all on so gigantic a scale that size lost significance. Against the towering cliffs the piñon trees looked like dwarfed shrubs."
David Lavender, *One Man's West*, 1956

"There are no eastern greens, no gentle contours, nothing soft, nothing easy. Hundreds of miles of rock scarcely blurred by vegetation, rib and vertebra without flesh, rock the color of dried blood, earth the color of old leather, scuffed and rutted, gullied and wrinkled. Most of the time even the sky is hard, such a vibrant, raucous blue, a color with such an edge to it that it is almost impossible to describe."
Ann Zwinger, *Wind in the Rock*, 1978

"Under a wine-dark sky I walk through light reflected and re-reflected from the walls and floor of the canyon, a radiant golden light that glows on rock and stream, sand and leaf in varied hues of amber, honey, whiskey—the light that never was is here, now, in the storm-sculptured gorge of the Escalante."
Edward Abbey, *Desert Solitaire*, 1968

Jeremy Schmidt: rock, tree, and sky, near Glen Canyon, Arizona.

William Neill: sandstone slot, near Glen Canyon, Arizona.

Collier/Condit: Rainbow Bridge (aerial), Utah.

" 'Zuni Nick, you've traveled all over these four corner States, worked for whites, and lived among the Navajo; what's the most wonderful thing you've ever seen?'

'Zuni Nick think the Great Cañon. But Navajo, he tell of thing he say much more great—Nonne-zoche Not-se-lid—he call it—that mean—Rainbow of Stone.'

'Where is that, Zuni Nick?'

'Oh, Zuni Nick never go there—far, far—hard on horses—no water—no food—nothing but rock and rock.' "

Clyde Kluckhohn, *To the Foot of the Rainbow*, 1927

"...we beheld before us a new and strange world: Rock, rock, rock; thousands upon thousands of red domes . . . The whole scene suggested a cubist painting.

. . . Accustomed as we had been to quaint perspectives, ancient ruins, phantasmagorial impressions of nomad life, mountain solitude, cañon depths, starry skies, and uninhabited wastes, this sudden view of a sea of gigantic, bare, iridescent, huddled planet tops, continuous as far as the eye could reach, was none the less appealing . . .

The stillness, the intense sense of physical loneliness, were overwhelming. The barrenness of this blasted region is terrible yet beautiful and wonderful.

. . . the scene was too much for a finite mind."

Clyde Kluckhohn, *To the Foot of the Rainbow*, 1927

"Geology here forever dominates life and gives it its ultimate meaning."

**Frank Waters,
The Colorado, 1946**

"...red dust, red sand, the dark smoldering purple reds of ancient rocks, Chinle, Shinarump and Moenkopi, the old Triassic formations full of radium, dinosaurs, petrified wood, arsenic and selenium, fatal evil monstrous things, beautiful, beautiful."
Edward Abbey,
Slickrock, **1971**

"Wherever we look there is but a wilderness of rocks,—deep gorges where the rivers are lost below cliffs and towers and pinnacles, and ten thousand strangely carved forms in every direction, and beyond them mountains blending with the clouds."
John Wesley Powell, *The Exploration of the Colorado River and its Canyons*, 1895

"In page after page Powell strove to describe a kind of landscape neither he nor any of his men had ever seen before. He came closer than anyone else to evoking through words the character of the canyonlands. Yet the strangeness of it can barely be suggested through language. In fact, the land can hardly be understood through the eyes. The imagination cannot comprehend what is so remote from all previous experience . . ."
Edward Abbey,
The Journey Home, **1977**

"The lover of nature, whose perceptions have been trained in the Alps . . . or New England, in the Appalachians . . . or Colorado, would enter this strange region with a shock, and dwell there for a time with a sense of oppression . . . But time would bring a gradual change. . . . Great innovations, whether in art or literature, in science or in nature, seldom take the world by storm. They must be understood before they can be estimated, and must be cultivated before they can be understood."
Clarence E. Dutton,
Tertiary History of the Grand Canyon District, **1882**

"But now, as I walked, I found myself looking at the rock more closely, thinking it more closely, feeling it more closely. It seemed as if all at once I could recognize, in some new and more thorough way—without any sense of revelation, just with an easy acceptance—how time, sandpapering rock, had created harmony and beauty. (But, after all, what was beauty but some kind of harmony between the rock and my senses?)
. . . It was very simple really. The only thing the wind and the dust needed was time.
And now I found that I was ready to grant them the time. For at last I could look, steadily, beyond today and tomorrow. And beyond yesterday. . . . I knew now how it had been."
Colin Fletcher,
The Man Who Walked Through Time, **1968**

William Neill: sandstone slot, near Glen Canyon, Arizona.

Tom Till:
Goblin Valley, Utah.

Paul Logsdon:
Fiery Furnace,
Arches National Park
(aerial), Utah.

Tom Till: La Sal Mountains and Behind-the Rocks, view from Geyser Pass, Canyonlands, Utah.

Stephen Trimble:
Wingate Sandstone,
The Castle, Capitol
Reef, Utah.

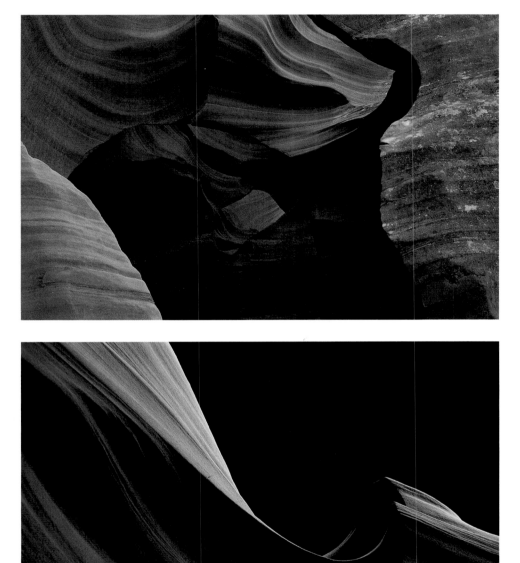

Jeremy Schmidt:
sandstone slot, near
Glen Canyon,
Arizona.

Jeremy Schmidt:
sandstone slot, near
Glen Canyon,
Arizona.

John Running:
Precambrian Vishnu
schist fluted by the
Colorado River,
Grand Canyon.

Stephen Trimble: sunset on desert varnish, Hyde's Wall, East Moody Canyon, Escalante Wilderness, Utah.

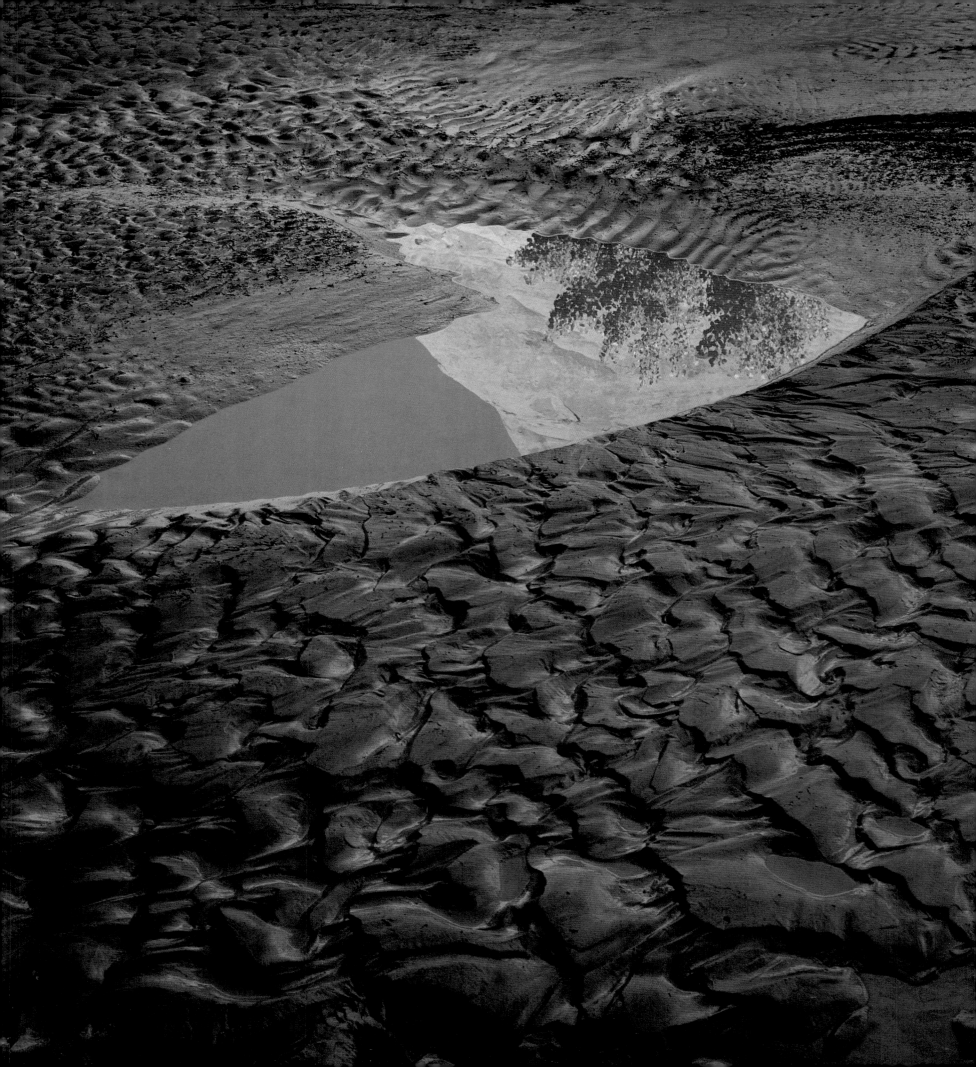

WATER

"Like a great soul in an unappreciative world, the Colorado runs its deep, silent, lonely course, too little understood, too little appreciated, loved by few, feared by many, and only a name to the multitudes who have never seen it."
Julius Stone, *Canyon Country*, **1932**

"The River . . . is an elemental force and perhaps too remote from human endeavor to be rightly comprehended. We test it by intellectual or economic standards and find it a great unconformity, an anomaly, an extravagance—something incomprehensible. We try to utilize it but it defies us. We think to make application of it in art and literature, but it does not respond. It is not classic, romantic, realistic, or cubistic. We can do little with it."
John Van Dyke, *The Grand Canyon of the Colorado*, **1920**

"To stick your hands into the river is to feel the cords that bind the earth together in one piece."
Barry Lopez, *River Notes*, **1979**

"We felt that we could overcome almost anything in the line of rapids the world might afford, and Steward declared our party was so efficient he would be willing to 'run the Gates of Hell' with them! Barring an absence of heat Cataract Canyon had been quite a near approach to that unwelcome entrance, and the locality of the mouth of the Dirty Devil certainly resembled some of the more favoured portions of Satan's notorious realm."
Frederick S. Dellenbaugh, *A Canyon Voyage*, **1926**

"Some observers have described the red water of the Little Colorado, others the slimy yellow water; still others, its limpid water. The observations were made at different times and doubtless all are correct."
Julius Stone, *Canyon Country*, **1932**

"That river. That river, that golden Green, flowing down from the snows of the Wind River Range, through Flaming Gorge and Echo Park, Split Mountain and The Gates of Lodore, down from the hills of Ow-Wi-Yu-Kuts, from the Yampa, Bitter Creek and Sweetwater, down the canyon called Desolation through the Tavaputs Plateau to emerge from the portal of the Book Cliffs—which

John Wesley Powell thought 'one of the most wonderful facades in the world'—and there to roll across the Green River Desert into a second world of canyons, where the river gives itself to Labyrinth and Stillwater and the Confluence with the Grand, under the rim of The Maze and into the roaring depths of Cataract. . . ."
Edward Abbey, *The Monkey Wrench Gang*, **1975**

Ira Estin: falls on Chinle Wash, Arizona.

Erica Wangsgard: Spring Canyon, Capitol Reef, Utah.

"...suddenly, swift and quiet and almost stealthy, running a strange milky blue over pebbles like gray jade, Havasu Creek comes out of nowhere across the trail, a stream thirty feet wide and knee-deep.

... There are in the West canyons as colorful and as beautiful as Havasu, with walls as steep and as high, with floors as verdantly fertile. . . . But I know of none . . . which has such bewitching water. In this country the mere presence of water, even water impregnated with red mud, is much. But water in such lavish shining streams, water so extravagantly colorful, water which forms such terraces and pools, water which all along its course nourishes plants that give off that mysterious wonderful smell like witch hazel, water which obliges by forming three falls, each more beautiful than the last, is more than one has a right to expect."
Wallace Stegner, *The Sound of Mountain Water*, 1969

"'I love all things that flow,' said James Joyce. 'If there is magic on this earth it lies in water,' Loren Eiseley said. And nowhere is water so beautiful as in the desert, for nowhere else is it so scarce. By definition. Water, like a human being or a tree or a bird or a song, gains value by rarity, singularity, isolation. In a humid climate, water is common. In the desert each drop is precious."
Edward Abbey, *Beyond the Wall*, 1984

"When side creeks are flooding, the river turns to chocolate and red, roiling with debris and extra power. The red dust gives the water a unique smell that is not instantly recognizable. Even immersion in water cannot take away its character.

This flooding Canyonlands river has an aroma like its paradoxical nature. It smells like the land it creates and destroys, like red rock baking in the sun. Its red waters smell like dryness."
Stephen Trimble, *The Sierra Club Guide to the National Parks of the Desert Southwest*, 1984

Jeremy Schmidt: Hidden Canyon, Arizona.

"There was a time when, in my search for essences, I concluded that the canyonland country has no heart. I was wrong. The canyonlands did have a heart, a living heart, and that heart was Glen Canyon and the golden, flowing Colorado River."
Edward Abbey, *Beyond the Wall*, 1984

"...the most beautiful place in all the region of Glen Canyon was a cavernous space, under vaulting rock walls, that had been named the Cathedral in the Desert. The great walls arched toward one another forming high and almost symmetrical overlapping parabolas. They enclosed about an acre of ground, in which had grown willows, grasses, columbine, and maidenhair fern. The center of this scene was a slim waterfall, no more than a foot in diameter, that fell sixty feet into a deep and foaming pool. From it a clear stream had flowed through the nave and out to the Colorado."
John McPhee, *Encounters With the Archdruid*, 1971

"It is reflection that imparts magic to the waters of the Glen Canyon and its tributaries. Every pool and rill, every sheet of flowing water, every wet rock and seep—these mirror with enameled luster the world about. In narrow chasms streams of melted gems flow over purple sand past banks of verdant willow. Small puddles, like shining eyes, fuse the colors of pink rocks and cerulean sky, and wet ripples of mud may do the same thing. In the changing light nothing remains the same from year to year or hour to hour. Flood and drouth, heat and cold, life and death alter the finer details incessantly, but they leave unchanged the grand plan . . ."
Eliot Porter, *The Place No One Knew: Glen Canyon on the Colorado*, 1963

"Dipping the oar gently in the glassy tongue above Crystal Rapids, time very nearly stops. Sunlight turns the water dripping off the blade into dazzling jewels while below the current churns into a thundering roar: but both go unnoticed. The oarsman concentrates to the point of total absorption, looking for a key wave or nub of rock marking the entrance into the rapids. When all of one's forces have been gathered to attention on that smooth entrance, there is no time, there is only an eternity in which we are poised . . ."
Larry Stevens, *Plateau Magazine*, 1981

"Running the big rapids is like sex: half the fun lies in the anticipation. Two-thirds of the thrill comes with the approach. The remainder is only ecstasy— or darkness."
Edward Abbey, *Beyond the Wall*, 1984

"Our life now was so strenuous every hour of the day that our songs were forgotten, and when night came every man was so used up that as soon as supper was over rest and sleep were the only things that interested us. Though our beds were as hard and rough as anything could be, we slept with the intensity of the rocks themselves, and it never seemed more than a few minutes before we were aroused by the Major's rising signal 'Oh-ho, boys!' and rose to our feet to pack the blankets in the rubber bags, sometimes with a passing thought as to whether we would ever take them out again."
Frederick S. Dellenbaugh, *A Canyon Voyage*, 1926

"...I would defy anyone, even at this late day, whatever his object may be, to make a journey by boat of twelve hundred miles through those still, weird chasms, and down that yet mysterious River, and not be brought under their influence. If he did, he would be a man without nerves, devoid of all poetic sentiment—a mere bag of bones."
Robert Brewster Stanton, *Down The Colorado*, 1965

"In the canyon itself the days flow through your consciousness as the river flows along its course, without a break and with hardly a ripple to disturb their smoothness. . . . The current becomes the time on which you move. Things happen and days pass. . . . You glide on into the day unpursued, living, as all good river travelers should, in the present."
Eliot Porter, *The Place No One Knew: Glen Canyon on the Colorado*, 1963

Gordon Anderson: Granite Falls, Grand Canyon of the Colorado River.

Stephen Trimble:
Crystal Rapid, Grand
Canyon of the
Colorado River.

Catherine Viele:
Woods Canyon,
Mogollon Rim,
Arizona.

Catherine Viele: Agate and Sapphire rapids from Tonto Trail, Grand Canyon of the Colorado River.

Philip Hyde: Colorado River at bend above Klondike Bar, Glen Canyon
(before flooding), Utah.

Philip Hyde: pool at Fronds Gelées Canyon, Glen Canyon (before flooding), Utah.

Philip Hyde: reflections, Escalante River, Utah.

Jeff Gnass:
waterfall, Zion
Canyon, Utah.

Stephen Trimble:
barberry leaf and
reflections,
Scorpion Gulch,
Escalante
Wilderness, Utah.

Mark Zarn:
Coyote Gulch,
Escalante
Wilderness, Utah.

CANYONS

"As we neared the eastern brink of the Colorado River Canyon the land grew rougher, wilder. Here is the beginning of that incredible epic of erosion which reaches its climax in Grand Canyon, Arizona. Yawning gorges split the earth. Water draining through these tortuous cracks often hews itself a brand-new channel. This leaves the old canyon isolated, a looping, senseless gouge in the landscape. Other canyons, junction-bound, swing close together with only a thin ridge a thousand feet high between them."

David Lavender, *One Man's West*, 1956

"Canyons, through which great rivers roll onward to the ocean, and whose walls rise up so high as to shut out the glare of day . . . all pale before the awful Gorge of the World, the Mu-kun-tu-weap valley of the Virgin river in southern Utah. . . . whose feet rest on the sward and whose brows confront the sky . . . dazzling in their barbaric splendor of color, their . . . scenes of magnificent disorder . . ."

H.L.A. Culmer, *The Scenic Glories of Utah*, 1909

"...away again along the canyon and the Virgin River (how sweet to see sweet water sweetly flowing here between these dizzy soapstone blocks of red) and round the bendings of the river by the soapstone walls of blank fierce red and into the valley floor and trees (a little like Yosemite, this valley, yet not so lush, so cool, nor so enchanted . . .

. . . so by the road down to the canyons end and all around the beetling blocks of soapstone red, and river flowing, and trees and shade . . . "

Thomas Wolfe, *A Western Journal*, 1938

Mary Allen: Fiery Furnace, Arches National Park, Utah.

"From the rim . . . its depths convey a sense of great stillness, of motionlessness. But riding the river, the canyon world *moves*.

. . . Floating the rivers takes you through the land, not merely over its surface. Entering a canyon is akin to entering the living body of the earth, floating with its lifeblood through arteries and veins of rock, tuning your perceptions to the slow pulse of the land, single beats of river current marking the steady rhythmic changes of geologic time."

Stephen Trimble, *The Bright Edge*, 1979

"The traveler on the brink may gaze from afar and be overwhelmed with the sublimity of massive forms. But the traveler in the gorges stands among them and of them, becoming, through fair companionship, part and parcel of the incomprehensible whole. . . . In reality we are twin brothers to the rocks!"

Julius Stone, *Canyon Country*, 1932

Dennis Turville:
The Narrows,
Zion Canyon, Utah.

David Ochsner: Marble Gorge, Grand Canyon.

"The heavenly bodies look so much more remote from the bottom of a deep cañon than they do from the level. The climb of the walls helps out the eye, somehow. I lay down on a solitary rock that was like an island in the bottom of the valley, and looked up. . . . The arc of sky over the cañon was silvery blue, with its pale yellow moon, and presently stars shivered into it, like crystals dropped into perfectly clear water."
Willa Cather, *The Professor's House*, 1925

"I discovered that . . . all canyons . . . have a powerful sense of direction and this becomes imprinted upon one's way of thinking: there are upcanyon and downcanyon, and one adjusts to that simple fact.

. . . I would like to think that I could be set down blindfolded in any one of these canyons and know where I was when I could see . . . For, beyond the obvious physical characteristics, one begins to have a feel for each canyon itself—its way of going, its way of defining the sky, its way of turning, that belongs to it alone."
Ann Zwinger, *Wind in the Rock*, 1978

"Apparently it was a flat world, after all, and here was the edge. I stared over these battlements and saw a few last snowflakes fall into misty space. . . . then, down there somewhere, there was a swirling, a lifting, a hint of some early creative effort in the mist of Time. The next moment what breath I had left was clean gone. I was looking into the Grand Canyon."
J.B. Priestley, *Midnight on the Desert*, 1940

"The reactions of people to the Grand Canyon are interesting. Most of them are honest. They just give up. There is nothing to say; it is there and it is to be experienced. The impact on the consciousness when a visitor takes a look from either rim for the first time is stunning. Charles F. Lummis put it succinctly in these words: 'I have seen people rave over it; better people struck dumb with it; even strong men who cried over it; but I have never yet seen the man or woman that expected it.' "
Edwin Corle, *Listen, Bright Angel*. 1946

"I think of the Canyon as first of all an exercise for the intelligence. . . . it gives me a kind of seasickness and sleeplessness— what I call cosmic vertigo. . . . It debunks the ego like nothing else."
Haniel Long, *Piñon Country*, 1941

...the canyon is nearly all rock. How much can you say about rock? It's red here, gray there, it's hard, it's badly eroded, it's a mess. The geologists can't even make up their minds how the canyon was formed. They once thought it was an entrenched meander, the ancient silt-bearing river grinding down into its bed as the plateau gradually rose beneath it. Now some think it's the result of two rivers, one capturing the other in the vicinity of the present Little Colorado. Old-time geologists spoke of a monster cataclysm. One thing is certain: the Grand Canyon is *the canyon*."
Edward Abbey, *Beyond the Wall*, 1984

Gordon Anderson: Toroweap, Grand Canyon of the Colorado.

"The Grand Canyon of the Colorado is a canyon composed of many canyons. It is a composite of thousands, of tens of thousands, of gorges. . . . it is a vast district of country. Were it a valley plain it would make a state. . . . You cannot see the Grand Canyon in one view, as if it were a changeless spectacle from which a curtain might be lifted, but to see it you have to toil from month to month through its labyrinths. . . . if strength and courage are sufficient for the task, by a year's toil a concept of sublimity can be obtained never again to be equaled on the hither side of Paradise."
John Wesley Powell, *The Exploration of the Colorado River and its Canyons*, 1895

"When I woke next morning a broad red band lay heavy along the eastern horizon. Already the black velvet had moved over into blue. Soon the shapes began. The red band diminished. The sun rose and broadcast thin, tentative beams. Two ravens planed past, craaaking; a woodpecker embarked on its day's bayoneting. The blue velvet eased over into gray. The shapes hardened into buttes and ridges. At last, almost imperceptibly, the gray velvet had become the Canyon."
Colin Fletcher, *The Man Who Walked Through Time*, 1968

"The great chasm cannot be successfully exploited commercially or artistically. It cannot be ploughed or plotted or poetized or painted. It is too big for us to do more than creep along the Rim and wonder over it. Perhaps that is not cause for lamentation. Some things should be beyond us—aspired to but never attained."
John Van Dyke, *The Grand Canyon of the Colorado*, 1920

Mark Zarn: Scorpion
Gulch, Escalante
Wilderness, Utah.

Stephen Trimble:
Monument Canyon,
Colorado National
Monument.

John Telford: Cow Canyon, Escalante Wilderness, Utah.

John Telford: Box Elder Park, Yampa River, Dinosaur National Monument, Colorado.

Jeff Gnass: sunrise from Maricopa Point, South Rim, Grand Canyon.

Jeff Gnass: sunrise, Mount Hayden from Point Imperial, North Rim, Grand Canyon.

MESAS

"Once again I had that glorious feeling that I've never had anywhere else, the feeling of being *on the mesa,* in a world above the world. And the air, my God, what air! Soft, tingling, gold, hot with an edge of chill on it, full of the smell of piñons—it was like breathing the sun, breathing the colour of the sky."
Willa Cather, *The Professor's House*, 1925

"...the heart of the inner Plateau Country . . . is a maze of cliffs and terraces lined off with stratification, of crumbling buttes, red and white domes, rock platforms gashed with profound cañons, burning plains barren even of sage—all glowing with bright colors and flooded with blazing sunlight. Everything visible tells of ruin and decay. It is the extreme of desolation, the blankest solitude, a superlative desert."
Clarence E. Dutton, *Geology of the High Plateaus of Utah*, 1880

"The sun is beginning to set, and at last my camp is in shadow. The desert still throbs with heat, but below in the canyon, frogs have begun to croak, heralding the cool approach of Night. I am a day's journey from Rainbow Bridge. Yesterday I came down the mountain, over a steep and rocky trail. . . .

Seen from the mountain, the country between here and the San Juan and Colorado rivers and beyond them is as rough and impenetrable a territory as I have ever seen. Thousands of domes and towers of sandstone lift their rounded pink tops from blue and purple shadows. To the east, great canyons seam the desert, cutting vermilion gashes through the grey-green of the sage-topped mesas."
Everett Ruess, letter from Navajo Mountain, Utah, June 30, 1934

"This mesa plain had an appearance of great antiquity, and of incompleteness; as if, with all the materials for world-making assembled, the Creator had desisted, gone away and left everything on the point of being brought together, on the eve of being arranged into mountain, plain, plateau. The country was still waiting to be made into a landscape.

. . . every mesa was duplicated by a cloud mesa, like a reflection, which lay motionless above it or moved slowly up from behind it. These cloud formations seemed to be always there, however hot and blue the sky. Sometimes they were flat terraces, ledges of vapour; sometimes they were dome-shaped, or fantastic, like the tops of silvery pagodas, rising one above another, as if an oriental city lay directly behind the rock. The great tables of granite set down in an empty plain were inconceivable without their attendant clouds, which were a part of them, as the smoke is part of the censer, or the foam of the wave."
Willa Cather, *Death Comes for the Archbishop*, 1927

Galen Rowell: Mitten Butte, Monument Valley, Arizona.

Tom Till: thunderstorm, San Rafael Reef, Utah.

"...ranks of stacks and mesas of Monument Valley . . . one of the purest diagrams of the Great American Desert View, precisely and completely consisting of a flat foreground and system of vertical backgrounds. . . . Monument Valley is our canonical image of America Deserta, exploited in a million television commercials, instantly recognizable even in the most simplified silhouette.

. . . Viewed from below—the normal human viewpoint for mesas—their sheer cragging verticality overwhelms the understanding. 'Forbidding' is a metaphor too casually applied to mountains . . . For practically half its height, the face of the mesa rises sheer and vertical—it must be something like three hundred feet of pure and uncompromised elevation, and if that does not 'forbid,' I don't know what does. And therefore the prohibited flat top is the natural abode of fantasies and mysteries, the calculated dreams of advertisers, and the gods of the dwellers on the plain below."
Reyner Banham, *Scenes in American Deserta,* **1982**

Diane Allen: Fajada Butte, Chaco Canyon, New Mexico.

"Monument Valley: red to blue; great violet shadows, planes and prisms of light.

. . . The valley is vast. When you look out over it, it does not occur to you that there is an end to it. You see the monoliths that stand away in space, and you imagine that you have come upon eternity. They do not appear to exist in time. You think: I see that time comes to an end on this side of the rock, and on the other side there is nothing forever. I believe that only in *dine bizaad,* the Navajo language, which is endless, can this place be described, or even indicated in its true character. Just there is the center of an intricate geology, a whole and unique landscape . . . The most brilliant colors in the earth are there, I believe, and the most beautiful and extraordinary land forms— and surely the coldest, clearest air, which is run through with pure light."
N. Scott Momaday,
***The Names,* 1976**

"We are now down among the buttes, and in a region the surface of which is naked, solid rock—a beautiful red sandstone, forming a smooth, undulating pavement. The Indians call this the *Toom'pin Tuweap',* or 'Rock Land,' and sometimes the *Toom'pin wunear' Tuweap',* or 'Land of Standing Rock.' "
John Wesley Powell, *The Exploration of the Colorado River and its Canyons,* 1895

". . .the colors are such as no pigments can portray. They are deep, rich, and variegated, and so luminous are they, that light seems to glow or shine out of the rock rather than to be reflected from it."
Clarence E. Dutton, *Geology of the High Plateaus of Utah,* 1880

"Low swells of prairie-like ground sloped up to the west. Dark, lonely cedar-trees, few and far between, stood out strikingly, and at long distances ruins of red rocks. Farther on, up the gradual slope, rose a broken wall, a huge monument, looming dark purple and stretching its solitary, mystic way, a wavering line that faded in the north. Here to the westward was the light and color and beauty. Northward the slope descended to a dim line of cañons from which rose an up-flinging of the earth, not mountainous, but a vast heave of purple uplands, with ribbed and fan-shaped walls, castle-crowned cliffs, and gray escarpments. Over it all crept the lengthening waning afternoon shadows."
Zane Grey, *Riders of the Purple Sage,*1912

"Here, at least, I shall haunt, and as the time-streams bend and swirl about the Rock, I shall see again all the times that I have loved, and know certainly all that now I guess at. I shall hear the drums far down in the dancing-place, and talk with feather-venders going up to Chaco and the cliff dwellings of Cañon de Chelly. . . . You, of a hundred years from now, if when you visit the Rock, you see the cupped silken wings of the argemone burst and float apart when there is no wind; or if, when all around is still, a sudden stir in the short-leaved pines, or fresh eagle feathers blown upon the shrine, that will be I, making known in such fashion as I may the land's undying quality."
Mary Austin, *The Land of Journeys' Ending,* 1924

Collier/Condit: West Canyon (aerial), Arizona/Utah.

Stephen Trimble: Enchanted Mesa, Acoma, New Mexico.

Stephen Trimble:
Factory Butte from
Fern's Nipple,
Capitol Reef, Utah.

Collier/Condit:
Cathedral Valley,
Capitol Reef
(aerial), Utah.

Stephen Trimble: The Castle, Capitol Reef, Utah.

Paul Logsdon: Monument Valley (aerial), Arizona/Utah.

Jeff Gnass: San Juan River Canyon and Monument Valley
from Muley Point, Utah.

Bruce Hucko: Great West Canyon, Zion National Park, Utah.

Mark Zarn: Monument Basin, Canyonlands (aerial), Utah.

PLATEAUS

"Once again I am in the desert that I know and love—red sand, twisted cedars, turquoise skies, distant mesas, and, far to the south, the blue line of the Mogollon Rim."
Everett Ruess, letter from Zeniff, Arizona, June 20, 1932

"I kept bright in my remembrance, as the very picture of things that are free, decent, sane, clean and true, what I had seen and felt—yes, even smelled—on that one blazing afternoon on a freight train rolling across the Southwest.

I mean the hot dry wind. The odor of sagebrush and juniper, of sand and black baking lava rock. I mean I remembered the sight of a Navajo hogan under a bluff, red dust, a lonesome horse browsing far away down an empty wash, a windmill and water tank at the hub of cattle trails radiating toward a dozen different points on the horizon, and the sweet green of willow, tamarisk and cottonwood trees in a stony canyon. There was a glimpse of the Painted Desert. For what seemed like hours I could see the Hopi Buttes, far on the north, turning slowly on the horizon as my train progressed across the vast plateau. There were holy mountains in the far distance. I saw gleaming meanders of the Little Colorado and the red sandstone cliffs of Manuelito. Too much. And hard-edged cumulus clouds drifting in fleets through the dark blue sea of the sky. And most of all, the radiance of that high desert sunlight, which first stuns then exhilarates your senses, your mind, your soul."
Edward Abbey, *Beyond the Wall*, 1984

"...the land drops off in broken ranges, along the Rim of the Mogollon Mesa. North of the Rim it lifts in alternate patches of grasslands and forest . . . Both the grass and the trees run with the wind in patterns that on a European map would measure states and empires, reduced by the whole scale of the country to intimacy. Once you have accepted the scale, it is as easy to be familiar with a grass-plot the size of Rhode Island or a plantation of yellow pines half as big as Belgium, as with the posy-plots of your garden."
Mary Austin, *The Land of Journeys' Ending*, 1924

Collier/Condit: Coal Mine Canyon area (aerial), Black Mesa, Arizona.

John Telford:
Sunset Point,
Bryce Canyon, Utah.

Stephen Trimble: moonset behind Hopi Buttes and Painted Desert, Petrified Forest, Arizona.

"One could not have believed that in the number of square miles a man is able to sweep with the eye there could be so many uniform red hills. He had been riding among them since early morning, and the look of the country had no more changed than if he had stood still. . . . They were so exactly like one another that he seemed to be wandering in some geometrical nightmare; flattened cones, they were, more the shape of Mexican ovens than haycocks—yes, exactly the shape of Mexican ovens, red as brick-dust, and naked of vegetation except for small juniper trees. And the junipers, too, were the shape of Mexican ovens. . . . The hills thrust out of the ground so thickly that they seemed to be pushing each other, elbowing each other aside, tipping each other over.

. . . there was so much sky, more than at sea, more than anywhere else in the world. The plain was there, under one's feet, but what one saw when one looked about was that brilliant blue world of stinging air and moving cloud. Even the mountains were mere ant-hills under it. Elsewhere the sky is the roof of the world; but here the earth was the floor of the sky. The landscape one longed for when one was far away, the thing all about one, the world one actually lived in, was the sky, the sky!"
Willa Cather, *Death Comes for the Archbishop*, 1927

". . .Painted Desert country and the Blue Forest . . . are like a million butterflies fluttering in the luminous air, over debris of tortoise-shell. They are like a million leopards leaping on a million zebras in a world of opal.

. . . Miles away on the horizon the high blue heads of mesas rest on sloping shoulders till the mirage guillotines them."
Haniel Long, *Piñon Country*, 1941

"Look west from the Canyon Country and you look up; hazy blue, forested heights rim the horizon. Mountains, no doubt, beyond the Plateau?

Almost. These forested walls bordering the western Canyon Country rise to summits high enough to qualify as mountains—nine thousand to over eleven thousand feet high—but they have flat tops: still plateaus. Not just plateaus, but the High Plateaus."
Stephen Trimble, *The Bright Edge*, 1979

"On top of the Wasatch Plateau, above nine thousand feet, the air is the kind that automobile tourists expect only on mountain passes. But there is no pass here, there are no peaks around us, only a rolling, grassy plain edged with rounding ridges covered with aspen and ponderosa pine. If this plain were in Nebraska, the horizon would spread to the limits of vision established by the earth's curvature. If it were in Montana, it would lift to the blue of distant mountains. But here we have the sense that just beyond any ridge the edge drops away. We are literally on a roof. It feels wonderfully high, open, sunny, and big. The wind blows off no contiguous land, but straight out of the sky."
Wallace Stegner, *American Places*, 1983

"...the barricades of Bryce . . . the least overwhelming, dizzy, and least massive of the lot—but perhaps the most astounding—a million wind-blown pinnacles of salmon pink and fiery white all fused together like stick candy—all suggestive of a child's fantasy of heaven . . . fragile compared to other great canyons . . . something the effect of sugar candy at a carnival—powdery—whitey— melting away . . . after last night's rain brightly amazingly pungent, sweet and fragrant— smell of sage, pine needles . . . ''
Thomas Wolfe, *A Western Journal*, 1938

"The Aquarius should be described in blank verse and illustrated upon canvas. . . . We have drawn nearer and nearer to it, and seen its mellow blue change day by day to dark somber gray, and its dull, expressionless ramparts grow upward into walls of majestic proportions and sublime import. . . . The mottling of light and shadow upon its middle zones is resolved into groves of *Pinus ponderosa,* and the dark hues at the summit into myriads of spikes, which we know are the storm loving spruces.

The ascent leads us among rugged hills . . . When the broad platform is gained the story of 'Jack and the beanstalk,' the finding of a strange and beautiful country somewhere up in the region of the clouds, no longer seem incongruous. Yesterday we were toiling over a burning soil, where nothing grows save the ashy-colored sage, the prickly pear, and a few cedars that writhe and contort their stunted limbs under a scorching sun. To-day we are among forests of rare beauty and luxuriance; the air is moist and cool, the grasses are green and rank, and hosts of flowers deck the turf like the hues of a Persian carpet."
Clarence E. Dutton, *Geology of the High Plateaus of Utah*, 1880

"...those who haven't the strength or youth to go into it and live can simply sit and look. They can look two hundred miles, clear into Colorado; and looking down over the cliffs and canyons of the San Rafael Swell and the Robbers' Roost they can also look as deeply into themselves as anywhere I know. And if they can't even get to the places on the Aquarius Plateau where the present roads will carry them, they can simply contemplate the *idea*, take pleasure in the fact that such a timeless and uncontrolled part of earth is still there.

. . . We simply need that wild country available to us, even if we never do more than drive to its edge and look in. For it can be a means of reassuring ourselves of our sanity as creatures, a part of the geography of hope."
Wallace Stegner, *The Sound of Mountain Water*, 1969

Collier/Condit: Antelope Canyon and San Francisco Peaks, Coconino Plateau (aerial), Arizona.

Stephen Trimble:
toward the Chuska
Mountains, near
Many Farms,
Arizona.

Stephen Trimble:
sunset over Mount
Taylor, New Mexico.

Collier/Condit:
ramparts, Lukachukai
Mountains (aerial),
Arizona.

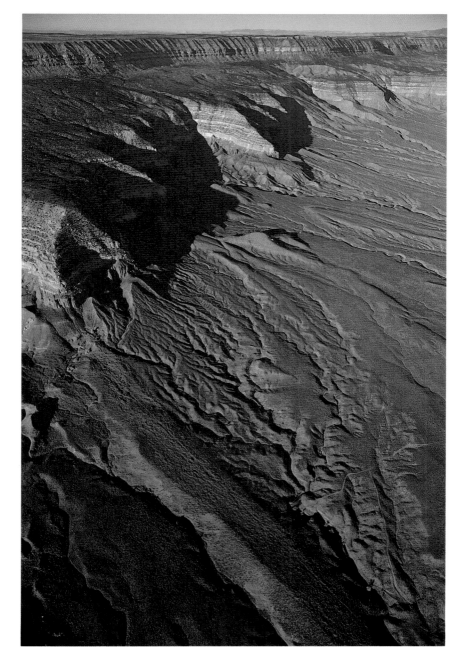

Collier/Condit:
Kaiparowits Plateau
(aerial), Utah.

Larry Ulrich:
Schnebly Hill,
Mogollon Rim, above
Sedona, Arizona.

Gordon Anderson:
sunset, Cedar Breaks,
Utah.

Philip Hyde: aspen, Kaibab Plateau, North Rim, Grand Canyon.

MOUNTAINS

"Most sacred is the bulk of Tsotsil, blue as a summer rainstorm . . . it rises from the mesa platform, a pyramidal, solitary mass of broken cones, from whose top, streams cloud like smoke of accepted sacrifice, following the high wind river. For a whole day's travel, east and west, it dominates the landscape to the north of the railway, a semicircular volcanic mass, having a secondary cone within, one clear creek, and a giant's tongue of black lava protruded down the shallow red sandstone cañon where the railway follows the old trail past Acoma to Zuñi. Tsotsil, it is called by the Navajo, in reference to the lava tongue, and, ceremonially, Blue Turquoise Mountain, sacred world altar of the South. But on the maps you will find it designated as Mt. Taylor.

. . . new mountains not yet worn down to the smoothed contours of maturity . . . crop out . . . south of Mt. Taylor, west of the Rio Grande, mountains unnamed and never lived in, blind cinder-heaps, cupped craters, wedged-shaped dikes surviving the cleft sandstone walls that shaped them. Dead mountains, dead and dreaming. Mostly it is water they dream of, as women unfulfilled are said to dream of the sea. Any way you look, traveling across that country, the dream comes stealing."
Mary Austin, *The Land of Journeys' Ending*, 1924

"They used a sunbeam to fasten *Dook'o'oosłííd* in the west to the firmament. Then they decorated it with haliotis shell. They decorated it with a variety of animals. It too they decorated it with the black clouds that produce the harsh, sudden male rain.

On the top of *Dook'o'oosłííd* in the west they placed a large bowl of haliotis shell. Into that bowl they placed two eggs of *Tsídiiltsooí* the Yellow Warbler, for they also wanted plenty of feathers on this mountain. Then they covered those eggs with a sacred buckskin to be sure that they would hatch. Which explains why so many yellow warblers live on that mountain to this day.

All that they had placed on *Dook'o'oosłííd* in the west they covered with a yellow cloud. And from material which they had obtained before they left the world below they fashioned *Naadą́ą́lgaii ashkii* the White Corn Boy and *Naadą́ą́ltsoii at 'ééd* the Yellow Corn Girl. These two they stationed to dwell there forever as the male god and as the female god of *Dook'o'oosłííd*, or San Francisco Peaks as it would now be called in the language that the White Man speaks."
Paul G. Zolbrod, *Diné Bahane': The Navajo Creation Story*, 1984

"The San Francisco Mountain lies in northern Arizona, above Flagstaff, and its blue slopes and snowy summit entice the eye for a hundred miles across the desert. About its base lie the pine forests of the Navajos, where the great red-trunked trees live out their peaceful centuries in that sparkling air.

. . . The great pines stand at a considerable distance from each other. Each tree grows alone, murmurs alone, thinks alone. They do not intrude upon each other. . . . Each tree has its exalted power to bear."
Willa Cather, *The Song of the Lark*, 1915

Jeff D. Nicholas: winter, La Sal Mountains from Devil's Garden, Arches National Park, Utah.

Gordon Anderson: Mount Mellenthin, La Sal Mountains, Utah.

"It is not, however, to watch the stars go by that the Navajo goes up to Dokoslid. From salient peak to peak of its broken mass, he renews the sense of the familiar which makes a man at home. North by west, he looks across the motionless streak of the Grand Cañon, past Kaibab and Kanab, to the home of the Utes; straight north, beyond the shadow which is the cañon of the Coloradito, dropping in a thin wide veil into the abysmal depth by which it reaches the Colorado Grande, to the phantom shape of Navajo Mountain, from whose north wall springs mysteriously the flying arch of Rainbow Bridge. Hereabout the first man was made, the original Navajo man."

Mary Austin, *The Land of Journeys' Ending*, 1924

"Down the river. Our boats turn slowly in the drift, we see through a break in the canyon walls a part of the Henry Mountains retreating to the northwest, last range in the United States to be named and explored and mapped. Mount Ellsworth, one of the lower peaks, is the one we see, rising sharp and craggy against the sky, a laccolithic dome of varicolored sedimentary and igneous rock (part of the intrusion now exposed by erosion) furred over with a growth of pinyon pine, juniper and jackpine at the highest elevations. The flowers we cannot see but easily imagine will also be blooming up there in the cool—larkspur, lupine, Indian paintbrush, the Sego lily, perhaps a few columbines."

Edward Abbey, *Desert Solitaire*, 1968

Philip Hyde: Abajo Mountains from Indian Creek, Canyonlands, Utah.

"...eastward across labyrinthine mazes of stone, rise the gray-green cones of the Henry Mountains, 'Gothic superimposed upon Byzantine,' a sharp contrast both in color and shape to the flat crestlines and predominant red of the surrounding desert, and absolutely lyrical when capped with snow. Beyond the Henrys the level desert platform, barren, blistered, cut by cliffs and canyons, reaches almost to the edge of vision, a hundred and fifty miles out, to the rich red rim of the world which we know to be the almost impenetrable country around the junction of the Colorado and the Green, in Canyonlands National Park. But above that desert rim rises another, farther outburst of Gothic—the snowy peaks of the La Sals, laccoliths like the Henrys, high cones of snow."

Wallace Stegner, *American Places*, 1983

"...why climb Tukuhnikivats? Because I prefer to. Because no one else will if I don't—and *somebody has to do it.* Because it is the most dramatic in form of the La Sals, the most conspicuous and beautiful as seen from my terrace in the Arches. Because, finally, I like the name. Tukuhnikivats—in the language of the Utes 'where the sun lingers.' "

Edward Abbey, *Desert Solitaire*, 1968

"[**S**hiprock's] . . . outline is so characteristic that it could serve as a graphic symbol or mascot for the area. Its isolation from all other mountains is conspicuous—they lie low on the horizons of all views of Shiprock, but none stands near, and its abrupt and pinnacled silhouette rises solitary from the broad ledges of the San Juan Valley, as unlikely as some German Expressionist structure.

. . . It rose, very properly for a desert mountain, from a wide stretch of nearly flat land, hard-baked clayish sand glowing white through the summer-dry sagebrush and grasses, sloping up at the base of the mountain to merge in both color and form into the more russet piers and ribs and buttresses . . .

In my immediate visual fantasy it appeared to have thrust up suddenly through the surface of the present plain, something new and almost man-made, with the striations and blemishes of manufacture still on its sides. A stranger, bluff and alert, in the land.

Sleeping Ute Mountain, by contrast, looks at home and at ease, like something that has, indeed, come to lie upon the land, not burst through it. . . . at great distances, it is immediately recognizable as Sleeping Ute, and one comes to welcome and respect it, to feel comforted by its amiable presence."

Reyner Banham, *Scenes in America Deserta*, 1982

"**T**he Sacred Mountains have always been where they are now.
They have been like that from the beginning.
They were like that in worlds before this.
They were brought up from the Underworld.
And were put back in their respective places.

When the mountains were replaced,
Earth was made.
Sky was made.
Dawn was made.

Earth is Our Mother.
Sky is Our Father.
Sun gives us light.
Moon does the same.
All of these were made for us to live by.

. . . These mountains and the land between them
Are the only things that keep us strong.
From them, and because of them we prosper. . . ."

George Blueeyes, *Between Sacred Mountains*, 1982

Collier/Condit: Shiprock (aerial), New Mexico.

Tom Till: rock glacier and aspens in fog, La Sal Mountains, Utah.

Tom Till: aspens just leafing out, Gold Basin, La Sal Mountains, Utah.

Stephen Trimble:
San Francisco Peaks
from the Painted
Desert, Arizona.

Collier/Condit:
sunset, Kendrick
Mountain from the
San Francisco Peaks
(aerial), Arizona.

Stephen Trimble: Henry Mountains and Waterpocket Fold, from Goosenecks Overlook, Capitol Reef, Utah.

Stephen Trimble:
winter, Sunset Crater,
Arizona.

Stephen Trimble:
Merriam Crater, San
Francisco Peaks
Volcanic Field,
Arizona.

TIME

"It is easy enough, of course, to grasp this story with your intellect. The difficulty comes when you try to accept its reality with your whole being.

. . . When I had sat and looked for a long time . . . Just for a moment I glimpsed the centuries reaching back and down into the Canyon and into the past, back and down through the corridor of time that stretches silently away behind us, back and down into the huge history that seems at first to leave no meaningful place for man.

And presently, when the fear had begun to subside . . . I saw that by going down into that huge fissure in the face of the earth, deep into the space and the silence and the solitude, I might come as close as we can at present to moving back and down through the smooth and apparently impenetrable face of time.

. . . all at once I was feeling, as if I had never understood it before, the swing and circle of the sun. Sunrise and sunset; sunrise and sunset; sunrise again; and then sunset. It happened everywhere, of course, all over the earth. But now I could detect in the beat of that rhythm an element I had never felt before. Now I could feel the inevitability of it. An inevitability that was impersonal and terrifying and yet, in the end, comforting."
Colin Fletcher, *The Man Who Walked Through Time*, 1968

"We wait on a ledge, balanced on the brink of an old canyon, seeing before us the first instant in the life of a new canyon. In this invisible moment between the long past and the unknown future, we stand on the edge, living on the rim of time."
Stephen Trimble, *Rim of Time: The Canyons of Colorado National Monument*, 1981

"The rhythm of the rocks beats very slowly, that is all. The minute hand of its clock moves by the millions of years. But it moves. And its second hand moves by the ceaseless eroding drip of a seep spring, by the stinging flight of sand particles on a gray and windy evening, by the particle-on-particle accretion of white travertine in warm blue-green waters—by the same ticking seconds that our watches record. And if you listen carefully—when you have immersed yourself long enough, physically and mentally, in enough space and enough silence and enough solitude— you begin to detect, even though you are not looking for it, something faintly familiar about the rhythm. You remember hearing that beat before, point and counterpoint, pulsing through the inevitable forward movement of river and journey, of species and isolated Indian community, of lizard and of flowering plant . . . And you grasp at last, in a fuller and more certain way than you ever have before, that all these worlds move forward, each at its own tempo, in harmony with some unique basic rhythm of the universe."
Colin Fletcher, *The Man Who Walked Through Time*, 1968

Tom Till: Hilltop Ruin and the North Rim, Grand Canyon.

William Neill: pictographs and desert varnish, Canyon del Muerto, Arizona.

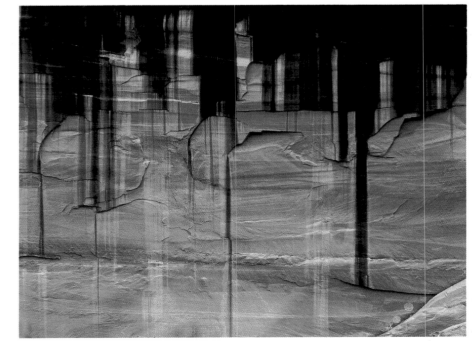

Stephen Trimble: side canyon waterfall, Cataract Canyon, Canyonlands, Utah.

"The narrow, damp, hidden worlds of the side canyons, with their scattered shards of Indian pottery and ghost imprints of 400-million-year-old nautiloids, open to the larger world of the Colorado River itself; but nothing conveys to us how far into the earth's surface we have come. Occasionally we glimpse the South Rim, four or five thousand feet above. From the rims the canyon seems oceanic; at the surface of the river the feeling is intimate. To someone up there with binoculars we seem utterly remote down here. It is this known dimension of distance and time and the perplexing question posed by the canyon itself—What is consequential? (in one's life, in the life of human beings, in the life of a planet)—that reverberates constantly . . . ''
Barry Lopez, *Plateau Magazine*, **1981**

"I wish I could tell you what I saw there, just *as* I saw it, on that first morning, through a veil of lightly falling snow. Far up above me, a thousand feet or so, set in a great cavern in the face of the cliff, I saw a little city of stone, asleep. It was as still as sculpture—and something like that. It all hung together, seemed to have a kind of composition: pale little houses of stone nestling close to one another, perched on top of each other, with flat roofs, narrow windows, straight walls, and in the middle of the group, a round tower.''
Willa Cather, *The Professor's House*, **1925**

"You walk in one of the winding cañons of southern Utah or Colorado, threaded by a bright stream, half smothered in choke-cherry and cottonwood, and suddenly, high and inaccessible in the cañon wall, the sun picks out the little windows in the walls amid the smoke-blue shadows, and you brush your eyes once or twice to make sure you do not see half-naked men, deer- and antelope-laden, climbing up the banded cliffs, and sleek-haired women, bright with such colors as they knew how to wring out of herbs and berries, popping in and out of the T-shaped openings like parakeets.''
Mary Austin, *The Land of Journeys' Ending*, **1924**

". . . her power to think seemed converted into a power of sustained sensation. She could become a mere receptacle for heat, or become a colour, like the bright lizards that darted about on the hot stones outside her door; or she could become a continuous repetition of sound, like the cicadas.''
Willa Cather, *The Song of the Lark*, **1915**

"Another day, and we were a little to the east of the mountain at a Navajo settlement called *tsa hogan*, or 'rock house' . . . It was a strange coincidence that on the morning when we said goodby to these, the last people we were to see for some time, both of our watches should stop.''
Clyde Kluckhohn, *To the Foot of the Rainbow*, **1927**

"**O**n the first day that Thea climbed the water-trail, she began to have intuitions about the women who had spent so great a part of their lives going up and down it. She found herself trying to walk as they must have walked, with a feeling in her feet and knees and loins which she had never known before—which must have come up to her out of the accustomed dust of that rocky trail. She could feel the weight of an Indian baby hanging to her back as she climbed.

. . . The stream and the broken pottery: what was any art but an effort to make a sheath, a mould in which to imprison for a moment the shining, elusive element which is life itself—life hurrying past us and running away, too strong to stop, too sweet to lose? The Indian women had held it in their jars."
Willa Cather, *The Song of the Lark*, 1915

"**T**he Anasazi, who gradually abandoned the scattered villages and great cultural centers on the northern plateau, did not simply walk out into the sands of the southern desert and disappear, vaporizing like the morning dew. . . . They . . . would never really vanish because they are a part of the genetic and mythic memory of men yet building pueblos of stone and adobe, women still shaping their pottery, and young boys learning their way into manhood in the kivas."
Donald G. Pike, *Anasazi: Ancient People of the Rock*, 1974

". . . **p**ictographs and petroglyphs alike, present an odd and so-far-untranslated language.

. . . The art served as a record. As practical magic. And as communication between wanderers. Water around the next bend, a certain zigzag sign might mean. We killed eleven bighorn here, only two hundred years ago, says a second. *We were here, say the hunters. We were here, say the artists.*

. . . It seems reasonable to suppose that the unknown people who left this record of their passage felt the same impulse toward permanence, the same longing for communion with the world that we feel today. To ask for any more meaning may be as futile as to ask for a meaning in the desert itself. What does the desert mean? It means what it is. It is there, it will be there when we are gone. But for a while we living things—men, women, birds, that coyote howling far off on yonder stony ridge—we were a part of it all. That should be enough."
Edward Abbey, *Beyond the Wall*, 1984

"**A**s for my own life, it is working out rather fortunately. These days away from the city have been the happiest of my life, I believe. It has all been a beautiful dream, sometimes tranquil, sometimes fantastic, and with enough pain and tragedy to make the delights possible by contrast.

. . . The world has seemed more beautiful to me than ever before. I have loved the red rocks, the twisted trees, the red sand blowing in the wind, the slow, sunny clouds crossing the sky, the shafts of moonlight on my bed at night. I have seemed to be at one with the world. I have rejoiced to set out to be going somewhere, and I have felt a still sublimity, looking deep into the coals of my campfires, and seeing far beyond them. I have been happy in my work, and I have exulted in my play. I have really lived.

. . . In the meantime, my burro and I, and a little dog, if I can find one, are going on and on, until, sooner or later, we reach the end of the horizon."
Everett Ruess, letter from Kayenta, Arizona, April 18, 1931

Tom Till: dunes and Agathla, Monument Valley, Arizona.

Mary Allen: Navajo
Sandstone landscape,
Arizona.

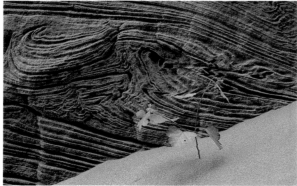

Jeremy Schmidt:
squawbush seedling,
Antelope Wash,
Arizona.

Jeff Gnass: The Tumbleweed Room, Arizona.

Stephen Trimble: doorways, Pueblo Bonito, Chaco Canyon, New Mexico.

Jeff D. Nicholas: Square Tower group, Hovenweep, Utah.

Jeff D. Nicholas:
window, Pueblo
Bonito, Chaco
Canyon, New
Mexico.

Greg Gnesios: petroglyphs, Indian Creek, Canyonlands, Utah.

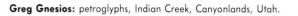

David Noble: pictograph, Natural Bridges, Utah.

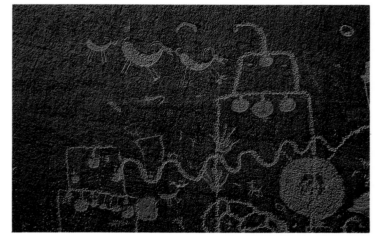

Stephen Trimble: petroglyphs, Hopi Clan Rocks, Arizona.

Ken Mabery: pictograph, The Needles, Canyonlands, Utah.

Larry Ulrich: Pueblo Bonito, Chaco Canyon, New Mexico.

AFTERWORD
PHOTOGRAPHING THE PLATEAU

One of the photographers contributing to *Blessed By Light,* John Running, is fond of a quote from Edward Steichen: "To see, to record, to comment, this is the work of documentary photography, to explain man to man and each man to himself."

I do not think Steichen would mind if I extended his observation to landscape: To see, to record, to comment, this is the work of landscape photography, to explain landscape to man and each man to himself.

The key to these parallel statements is *seeing.* And the results are the same: personal knowledge rooted in universal experience. There is no mention of art. That is a word for critics. Photographers make photographs, and that craft—one way of attempting to see into the landscape and into ourselves—is sufficient challenge.

Such personal journeys propel the photographers in this book out onto the Colorado Plateau. Most of us are in our thirties and forties. We came to the land as park rangers, teachers, river guides, naturalists, and backpackers. Most came in our youth, fresh from the 1960s, our idealism turned inward, searching for something, ready to grow up. Our photographs grew from these journeys.

The wild canyons gave us (and many others) what we searched for, and drew us back time after time. Some moved to the plateau. A few grew into self-taught photographers capable of bringing back images that captured what they learned to see and feel out there. Some now make their living at photography, but most of those do so because it lets them be in the wilderness, not because it is lucrative.

But we worry. Is it right to reveal these wild and fragile places? Do we want to invite in ever more people by publishing these photographs? We risk, in Philip Hyde's words, watching the land "be loved to death, even before being developed to death." We worry, but we believe it has to be done. We cannot afford to lose any more Glen Canyons because they were "places no one knew."

These photographs span twenty-five years of walking, river-running, and bouncing along back roads by the twenty-eight people who created them. They begin chronologically and spiritually with Philip Hyde's photo of the Colorado River at Klondike Bar in Glen Canyon, a place that no longer exists, today drowned by Lake Powell.

Phil Hyde came first. The rest of us went out with eyes trained by looking at Sierra Club books by Hyde and by Eliot Porter, and with our spirits roused by Edward Abbey's books *Desert Solitaire* and *The Monkey Wrench Gang.* We walked and camped and tried to see. The Colorado Plateau gives generously in exchange for our efforts. Its golden sandstone and days of clarity and stillness are there for everyone. Its land is blessed by light.

Photographing the Colorado Plateau is both easy and challenging. To obtain beautiful "calendar pictures" about all you have to do is point your lens into the overwhelming scenery and push the shutter release. The naked rock is full of abstractions, and an infinite number of tightly composed details hides in every side canyon.

But when we invited photographers to submit for *Blessed by Light,* we asked for images that had a metaphorical quality, that captured the iridescent plateau light. We considered some five thousand transparencies. We were looking for the hardest scenes to catch with a camera—great spaces and panoramas with their magic intact, pictures that transcend the literal.

The technical details behind these

photographs do not reveal much. Some of the transparencies came from large-format view cameras, some are 35-mm Kodachromes. All are sharp, properly exposed, and composed with care. Most were taken with tripods. The photographers favor sunrise and sunset light.

None of this explains the magic. True, you have to be a skilled enough technician to not let the fleeting few seconds of blazing light just before sunset get away. Transporting yourself and your twenty pounds of equipment to the place where that can happen is something else again.

These photographers have lived out there for days and weeks. Most know the plants and animals and rock formations, the archaeology and history. They know how the rivers and canyons and mesas fit together on maps. They know the books we quote from in *Blessed by Light.* Everything they know about themselves and the land is distilled in their photographs.

It is the land that counts most. Beyond its importance simply because it is there, a part of "the geography of hope," it counts because of what it can give to the humans who venture into it.

And so these photographs tell us about the Colorado Plateau, but they also tell us about the photographers. The pictures move the viewer because they communicate emotion. They carry the exhilaration and satisfaction felt by their makers at the time they saw these images.

The pictures carry the magic, but the magic *lives* out there in the plateau. As Edward Abbey says in his foreword: "Come on in and see for yourself."

Stephen Trimble

Paul Logsdon

Photographing from the air reveals the true scale of the plateau. From his home in Santa Fe, Paul Logsdon flies all over the Southwest, photographing from the pilot's seat of his small plane. A major portfolio of his work appears in *New Mexico: The Essential Landscape,* and his photographs of Anasazi ruins appear in *Exploration* magazine each year.

Ken Mabery

Trained as a geologist, currently a manager in the Santa Fe regional office of the National Park Service, Ken Mabery has been chief ranger at Chaco Canyon and El Morro. But his heart is in Canyonlands, where he worked for five years in the park's backcountry. In his youth he helped his father Slim (a ranger at Arches) scout the land that became Canyonlands National Park.

Steve McDowell

Eliot Porter's Glen Canyon book first sent New Mexican Steve McDowell to the canyons. Looking at it "formed a powerful impulse to go there, at the same time that I realized you could no longer see these places. It made me want to see what was left." He made his first extended plateau trip in 1976, when he did his first work in color. The canyons and color film proved a "delightful combination—a decadent combination." Steve worked for the Forest Service for many years, including fire tower jobs in New Mexico and boundary lines surveys for Manti-La Sal Forest in Utah. He now lives in Santa Fe.

William Neill

Native Californian Bill Neill spent five years as photographer for the Ansel Adams Gallery in Yosemite, where he still lives. Trained in environmental conservation, he has worked with the National Park Service and as a photography instructor. He uses a large-format camera primarily and is active in the world of exhibitions and galleries. Bill's roots may be in Yosemite, but he travels out onto the plateau each year, and the desert has become his second home. He is beginning work on a book of photographs that will communicate the power of Nature as healer.

Jeffrey David Nicholas

Jeff Nicholas' fascination with the desert started with a trip to Arizona from his home in Los Angeles when he was seven. Beginning in the 1970s, he came to the plateau to explore and photograph. With a background in architecture and fine arts, he has focused on ruins and rock art. The 1986 calendar *Anasazi: An American Civilization* featured his photographs. Jeff says of the plateau: "The magic I have experienced there is a core of warmth that I can never un-experience." He lives in Yosemite, where he works with The Ansel Adams Gallery.

David Grant Noble

Writer and photographer David Noble works for the School of American Research in Santa Fe, where he edits the journal *Exploration* and serves as director of public information. His books include *New Light on Chaco Canyon* and *Ancient Ruins of the Southwest: An Archaeological Guide.* He sums up his interest in archaeology: "Ruins are time anchors, giving substance to an elusive past."

David Ochsner

David Ochsner has worked for the National Park Service from Olympic to Mesa Verde to the Blue Ridge Parkway, but he spent the 1970s at the Grand Canyon. As natural resource specialist, he devoted considerable time to the park backcountry, and his photographs demonstrate that. Of the Grand Canyon, he says: "Don't enter it with preconceptions, either as a person or a photographer." Dave now works at Santa Monica Mountains in California, and also has been photographing the stone monuments of Easter Island.

Galen Rowell

Galen Rowell's expertise in both mountaineering and wilderness photography has resulted in a series of books, including *High and Wild; In the Throne Room of the Mountain Gods; Many People Come, Looking, Looking;* and *Mountains of the Middle Kingdom.* As a photographer, light counts most to him: "Photos are made of light, not things." Base camp is Albany, California, not far from where he started his wilderness trekking, in the Sierra.

John Running

From his studio and gallery in Flagstaff, Arizona, John Running photographs all over the world, from Palestinian people in Lebanon, to the hill towns of Tuscany, to the Tarahumara Indians of Mexico. Even so, hardly a year goes by when he fails to row his raft down the Colorado River in Grand Canyon. His most recent book is *Honor Dance: Native American Photographs.* In that book John says, "When I make pictures . . . I try to make an exchange. I have to leave something of myself behind."

Jeremy Schmidt

Another photographer and writer with roots as a park ranger, Jeremy Schmidt lives in the ponderosa pines outside of Flagstaff, Arizona. He has worked as winterkeeper in Yellowstone, and contributes many pieces to the Canadian magazine *Equinox*—with Chinese New Year in Tibet and elephant boys in Thailand next on his schedule. His books include *Snow Country* and *Adventuring the Rockies.* Jeremy wrote about sandstone "slots" in *Audubon* in 1978, likening hiking into them to being "inside the pumpkin."

John Telford

Well known for his ten years of black-and-white photography of the Great Salt Lake, collected in a 1979 portfolio, John Telford began photographing on the plateau in 1976. He had believed that "serious" photography had to be black-and-white, but "the country changed me. Black-and-white could not express what I was seeing and feeling there." He began to secretively use color film, and now uses it almost exclusively. In his urban life he teaches photography and directs the department of photographic services at the University of Utah.

Tom Till

Tom Till has lived in Moab, Utah for eleven years. Wintering as a teacher of high school journalism and photography, he has ranged across the Southwest with his cameras, hiking, exploring, and river-running. The summer of 1986 marks his shift to photographing full-time, and his projects include books on Canyonlands and Grand Canyon national parks; a book of aerial photos of Colorado; and a photographic odyssey in the steps of Clarence Dutton.

Stephen Trimble

A Colorado native, Stephen Trimble began photographing and writing about the plateau as a park ranger at Arches and Capitol Reef in the early 1970s. He later worked as publisher of the Museum of Northern Arizona Press, where he edited *Plateau* magazine. Steve has written some twenty-five articles and books about the plateau, including *Canyon Country* (with photographs by Dewitt Jones), *The Bright Edge: A Guide to the National Parks of the Colorado Plateau,* and *The Sierra Club Guide to the National Parks of the Desert Southwest.* He currently is working on books about Pueblo Indian pottery and contemporary Southwest Indian people and their landscape. He lives near Santa Fe, New Mexico.

Dennis Turville

From his home town of Salt Lake City, Dennis Turville ranges to Peru and Canada as a mountain guide. He saw Arches before the roads were paved, and some of the Glen Canyon country before flooding. He says, "The plateau is a state of mind rather than a place. The mountains challenge me, but the plateau keeps me sane." He is working on a book about his personal experiences in canyon country, while he supports himself with eighteen part-time jobs, most of which involve writing and photography.

Larry Ulrich

Californian Larry Ulrich began photographing because he thought it would be a way to support his fanatical love for trout fishing. He doesn't fish much anymore, but he photographs more than ever. In partnership with his wife Donna, he works all over the West from their base in Trinidad, California. Describing himself as a "latent geologist," Larry loves the canyon country because the "geology is right there." As for Donna, "If it were up to her, we would spend all of our time there." They don't, for their publishing projects include books on Arizona, Oregon, and northern California, as well as their *American Deserts* calendar.

Catherine Viele

Trained as an anthropologist, Cathy Viele's books include *Voices in the Canyon,* which grew from her time as a park ranger at Navajo National Monument, and *Moving Through the Seasons: The Southern Paiute People.* After ten years in Flagstaff, working as a Grand Canyon river guide, archaeologist, and local history columnist, she has become a temporary refugee from the Southwest in her native state of Maine. She lives on an island near Portland.

Erica Wangsgard

Erica Wangsgard moved to Salt Lake City from New York in 1976, discovered Escalante country the next year, and was "hooked." Beyond the "emotional, spiritual relationship with the land, visually it's a perfect place for me." She is finishing an M.F.A. in photography at the University of Utah, where she has focused on hand-colored black-and-white prints of abstract and intimate details from the plateau. "Each time I go down to southern Utah I see something new in the rock."

Mark Zarn

Mark Zarn came to the Southwest to do graduate work in biology, and moved to Denver where he wrote a series of reports on endangered and threatened species for the BLM and from where he discovered the canyon country in the 1970s. With his son's car seat bolted to the rowing frame of their raft, Mark and his wife row the San Juan River each spring. In between river trips, he lives in Conifer, Colorado, where he makes hand-crafted furniture.